The Forgotten Arts

YESTERDAY'S TECHNIQUES ADAPTED TO TODAY'S MATERIALS

by Richard M. Bacon

BOOK TWO

Published MCMLXXV by
YANKEE, INC.
Dublin, New Hampshire
03444

This Book Has Been Prepared by the Staff of Yankee, Inc.

Clarissa M. Silitch, Editor
Carl F. Kirkpatrick, Art Director

First Edition
Copyright 1975, by Yankee, Inc.
Printed in the United States of America

Fifth Printing, 1978

Library of Congress Catalog Card No. 75-10770
ISBN-0-911658-66-1

Contents

Foreword 5

Fireplace Cookery 6

Keeping Sheep for Meat, Wool, and Pleasure 12

Digging and Stoning a Well 18

How to Build a Smokehouse 24

Coping with a Whole Pig 29

Simple Wooden Toys that Last 35

Making Paint from Scratch 41

Decorating a Wall with Old-Fashioned Stenciling 45

How to Make an Apple-Picking Ladder 52

Keeping Geese, Guinea Hens, and Peacocks 57

Foreword

When uncertainty grips our lives, when familiar values seem to shift and crumble, an instinctive yearning for the traditional stability of the land persists among people beset by mounting pressures. Partly through nostalgia for an age that is only half-remembered, some think a move to the country will help re-establish a personal identity lost in a world of strangers.

Transplanting one's family is always hard. Learning to lead a life of partial self-sufficiency in the country — where deadlines tend to be seasonal and the pace is usually determined by the weather — can be an engulfing experience for those who are new to it. It takes time and understanding and an endless will to experiment. The land can still provide a portion of our food, our shelter, our clothing, and our entertainment. But even in a changed environment we tend to hang on to our established ways as tightly as a terrier locks his jaws around the neck of an offending woodchuck.

Confidence comes with experience. We know there is no real security. Nor is there any permanent escape from either pressure or ourselves no matter where we have an opportunity to live. We must learn again old ways, try our strengths, enjoy shared adventures, and face change.

Portents abound that we must develop a stronger independence of the spirit in the years ahead. Even in an uncertain, shifting world we can cultivate our inner resources, for here is fertile ground on which to broadcast the seeds of tomorrow's contentment.   *R. M. B.*

Fireplace Cookery

COOKING IN THE FIREPLACE IS NOT a difficult art to learn even if you have no experience and none of those venerable fireplace accessories like cranes, spits, spiders, skewers, jack clocks, and Dutch ovens so abundant in colonial kitchens and so expensive in today's antique shops. A few utensils are necessary but most of the necessary equipment can be found in your kitchen. The rest can easily be improvised while someone is getting the fire started.

You need: a grate or hinged metal grill like a hot-dog cooker for broiling; a roll of heavy-duty aluminum foil; an iron skillet with a close-fitting lid for stewing or baking; an earthenware casserole; a drip pan for catching the juices from roasts; a meat thermometer; some noncombustible butcher's twine, and a supply of dry firewood or charcoal.

Use birch or any hardwood for a good cooking fire, but wait until the fire has burned down to an overall glow with very little flame before starting to cook over it. (The same applies to charcoal.)

Fireplace cooking can be used for much more than just frying or grilling fish or meats (chops, steaks, hamburgers) or wrapping potatoes in aluminum foil packages to cook on top of a grill. Nearly anything prepared on the kitchen range or in its oven can be cooked before an open fire indoors, although a little more time (15 minutes to a half hour more than oven cooking) will be required.

Thus, an unexpected power failure need not prevent you from serving the same menu you were planning before the lights went out. If, for instance, you were planning

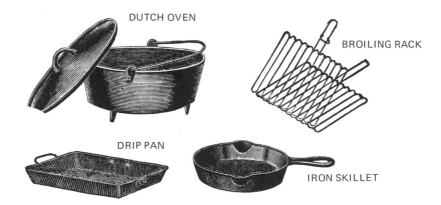

DUTCH OVEN

BROILING RACK

DRIP PAN

IRON SKILLET

Handy utensils for fireplace cookery

an oven-cooked meal—a casserole, stew or roast—for the main course, start your fire and make a "quick-and-easy" reflecting oven. Use a cookie sheet or find a board about 2 feet long and 1-1/2 feet wide. Cover it with aluminum foil to reflect the heat and prevent the board from catching fire. With bricks or a short log, prop the reflector in front of the fire so you can adjust it to a nearly perpendicular angle. Then, with sheets of foil make vertical "wings" along each end of the board and seal a narrower piece across the top (see p.8).

In the early 19th century, reflecting ovens were made of tin and included interior spits and hooks from which small game birds or skewer meats could be suspended—similar to the modern rotisserie.

The Dutch oven is another kind of roasting device. This was either a built-in feature at one side of the fireplace (with or without a hinged metal door) or an iron pot with a close-fitting and slightly concave lid on which to heap live coals. If you have a heavy iron frying pan but no lid, you can construct an adequate Dutch oven by covering the pan with several thicknesses of foil sealed around the perimeter.

With only a few basic utensils and some forks, spoons or ladles, you can serve a wide variety of meals. Here are several sample dinners that can be altered to suit your taste.

Scalloped Potato and Ham Casserole
or **Stew**
Canned Vegetables
Irish Griddle Scones
Cupcakes and Coffee

Main dish: Prepare your casserole

7

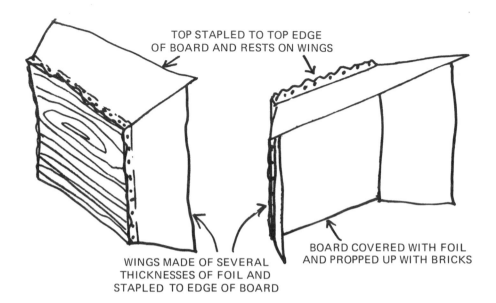

TOP STAPLED TO TOP EDGE
OF BOARD AND RESTS ON WINGS

BOARD COVERED WITH FOIL
AND PROPPED UP WITH BRICKS

WINGS MADE OF SEVERAL
THICKNESSES OF FOIL AND
STAPLED TO EDGE OF BOARD

Homemade reflecting oven

as usual and place it covered on the hearth within a reflecting oven. Rotate it 3 or 4 times to assure even cooking. Time: about 1-1/2 hours.

To make a stew, brown or braise your meat in oil with onions in an iron skillet or heavy frying pan on a bed of hot coals. Add liquid, vegetables, and seasoning. Cover and place the skillet in the reflecting oven. The time will be about the same as if you had cooked it in the kitchen oven.

Vegetables: Canned corn, beans, peas, carrots, etc., can be drained, seasoned and sealed in individual aluminum foil packages and placed on the hot coals until hot. Or put vegetables into an earthenware casserole to warm on a bed of hot coals that have been raked out to one side of the hearth.

Irish Griddle Scones: (4 cups flour, 1 teaspoon each sugar, baking soda, and salt. Add 2 cups milk and knead lightly for 5 minutes. Pat into rounds 1/2-inch thick). Preheat the frying pan by setting in on hot coals. Place the scones in it and cook about 7 minutes on each side. Butter and serve.

Cupcakes: While you are eating the main course, preheat your Dutch oven by burying it in the fire and heaping the lid with live coals. Pour the batter into a greased six-muffin tin. Place the tin in the Dutch oven, cover, and reheap the lid with coals. Cook 20-25 minutes. Sprinkle brown sugar on the cupcakes when cooked, and with firetongs pass a hot ember back and forth above them to melt or glaze the sugar.

The use of aluminum foil is a bow to modern convenience. In colonial times, of course, other packaging materials were used. Parchment was common. The Indians soaked green corn husks and wrapped them around food to be cooked. In other cultures cabbage leaves that had been wilted in boiling water for a few minutes or grape or papaya leaves were used to make envelopes. However, today it is easier and quicker to use foil.

For a good cup of coffee, if the power failure has caught you without either instant or a drip pot, try this recipe:

 1 cup coffee
 1 cup cold water
 1 egg
 6 cups boiling water

Beat the egg slightly. Dilute it with 1/2 cup cold water, add crushed egg shell, and mix with coffee. Pour into a pot, add boiling water and stir. Place the pot on hot coals and boil 3 minutes. If only heated and not boiled, the coffee will be cloudy; if boiled too long, tannic acids will develop and make it bitter. If you are using a coffee pot rather than a saucepan, pour some coffee into a cup to make sure the spout is free from grounds. Return the coffee to the pot and repeat. Add the remaining cold water (to perfect clarification) and let the pot stand for 10 minutes on the hearth where it will stay hot but not boil.

Planked fish is easy to prepare before an open fire. This need not be so hot a fire as you require for cooking meats, for fish should cook slowly and evenly. The taste will be entirely different from anything normally prepared on today's kitchen range.

Here is a sample menu with fish:

Planked Fish
(Mackerel, Salmon, Trout, etc.)
Vegetables
(Potatoes, Onions, Tomatoes)
Biscuits and Baked Bananas

Remove the head and tail from a whole fish, split lengthwise, butterfly, and tie in several places, skin side down, to a foil-covered reflecting board or cookie sheet. Brush with butter or oil, sprinkle with salt, pepper, and such herbs as fennel and lemon balm. Prop the plank at a steep angle before a fire that has burned down to glowing coals. Brush several times with melted butter or oil. When the flesh flakes easily, it is done. Time: about 35 minutes.

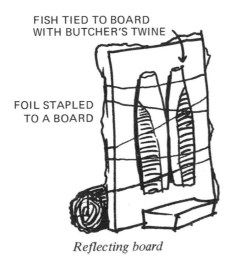

FISH TIED TO BOARD WITH BUTCHER'S TWINE

FOIL STAPLED TO A BOARD

Reflecting board

9

Vegetables: Wrap potatoes and peeled onions separately in double thicknesses of foil and seal. Place on top of coals and turn several times while cooking. Time: 35 minutes. Halve, salt and pepper whole tomatoes (add a pinch of fresh or dried basil) before sealing in double foil. Time: 10 minutes.

Biscuits: Make a biscuit batter and follow the procedure for cooking cupcakes.

Bananas: Line up whole bananas in their peels on the hearth before the fire. Turn once. When the skins are black (about 6 minutes), split them open lengthwise, sprinkle with sugar and cinnamon (a dash of rum can be added at this point) and eat them from the skins with a spoon.

Pictures of a colonial fireplace seem always to include a succulent roast in the foreground. You can serve a praiseworthy roast from the hearth with no more equipment than a piece of butcher's twine, a drip pan, and a homemade reflecting oven. Horizontal spits were used in earlier times. Later, meat was suspended on vertical-type spits and operated by boys or trained dogs, clockwork jacks, or a heat vane that rotated the meat by means of the hot draught in the chimney. But today, hang the roast on a string attached to the damper handle. Its weight will cause the meat to rotate with only occasional help from the cook. The drip pan will catch the juices and be handy for roasting potatoes.

Truss the meat (beef, lamb, ham, fowl, or wild game) with butcher's twine (meat shrinks in the cooking process) and suspend it before the fire within the reflecting oven.

Leg of Lamb (5 lbs. with bone)
Ash-Cooked Potatoes
Grilled Peppers
Acorn Squash
Johnny Cake
Apple Upside-Down Cake

Salt and pepper a bone-in leg of lamb at room temperature. Insert several slivers of garlic clove in the meat. With a trussing needle or skewer, thread a piece of butcher's twine through the small end of the roast, and insert a meat thermometer for accuracy. Hang it over a pan so it is suspended 6 inches to 8 inches from a hot fire and 2 inches above the hearth. Place the reflecting oven around it, wind the string occasionally. It will be ready to serve in about 2 hours.

Potatoes: Either cook peeled, cut-up potatoes in the drip pan for about 1-1/2 hours, turning occasionally, or bury unpeeled potatoes in the ashes to one side. Heaped with coals, they will be done in 75 to 90 minutes.

Acorn or Winter Squash (or any vegetable with a thick skin) can also be cooked in the ashes for about 60 minutes.

Grilled Peppers: Stick whole green peppers on a roasting fork or skewer and turn until completely charred. The skin can then be easily removed. Quarter and serve with butter, salt, pepper, and a little oil.

Johnny Cake: This can be cooked on a foil-covered board or cookie sheet at one side of the fire. To prevent the cakes from sliding, the batter will have to be thicker than usual. Make the batter by combining 1 egg, 1/2 teaspoon salt, 1/4 cup sugar, 1 teaspoon baking powder, 1

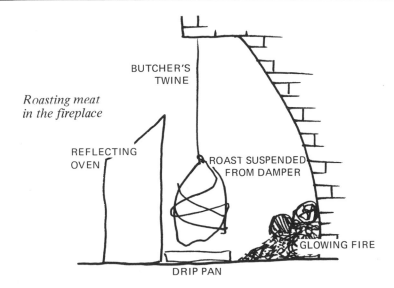

Roasting meat in the fireplace

BUTCHER'S TWINE

REFLECTING OVEN

ROAST SUSPENDED FROM DAMPER

GLOWING FIRE

DRIP PAN

cup flour, 1 cup cornmeal, with enough milk to make a stiff dough. Stir together. Form into cakes 1/2 inch thick and place them on the board near the fire so they can dry out and set slightly. When they have set, prop the board at an angle before hot coals. Adjust it as the cakes nearest the heat begin to brown. It is not necessary to turn the cakes themselves. In about 20 minutes split, spread with butter or honey, and serve.

Apples: Can be baked. Core, fill with brown sugar, raisins and a pat of butter. Then wrap and seal in double thicknesses of foil. Lay them in hot coals under the burning logs for about 30 minutes.

Another fireplace apple dessert is an upside-down cake. As you pre-heat the lid of an iron frying pan, spread 4 tablespoons butter on the bottom of the pan. Pare and slice enough apples to cover the bottom, sprinkle them with 1/2 cup sugar

and 1 teaspoon cinnamon. Pour on a batter made with 1 cup flour sifted with 1-1/2 teaspoons baking powder, 1/2 teaspoon salt, 1/4 cup butter and 1/2 cup sugar. Add 1 egg and then the dry ingredients to 1/2 cup milk and 1 teaspoon vanilla. Now rake out enough hot coals to one side of the fire to make a bed about 2 inches thick. Level the pan on them and cover. Heap the top with coals and bank the sides of the pan. Time: about 1 hour.

There are many other vegetables that can be cooked before an open fire without being boiled. Variety depending on the season will provide balanced and interesting meals. And any meal is complemented by a fresh salad. Without the pressure of an emergency such as a power failure, a little prior experience in timing is all that will be needed to turn out from the fireplace a gourmet meal of several courses featuring different sauces and beverages.

Keeping Sheep for Meat, Wool, and Pleasure

SHEEP RAISING NEED NOT BE A BIG business. Here in New England, a flock of from three to a dozen ewes and a ram, properly managed, can be self-sustaining and more economical to keep than most farm animals. Such flocks provide meat, wool, and pleasure. They combat second growth in the pasture and help maintain open space. Once the household needs have been met, surplusage can be bartered or sold to neighbors and craftsmen.

Traditionally, the farm flock is bred to produce a crop in the early spring, after the coldest weather is over and before summer heat comes to encourage parasites and discomfort. After being shorn, the sheep are turned out to pasture to fend for themselves all summer. Come fall, the ram is reintroduced to the ewes, and the cycle begins again.

Before the pasture greens, the homesteader will have experienced lambing. This is the high point of his career as a shepherd, when more and more time will need to be spent in the sheep barn checking the condition of the ewes day and night.

Sheep have the reputation of being difficult and dumb—especially when about to lamb, but others in the barnyard deserve these epithets more. Some ewes will appreciate a helping hand, particularly if it is a first or multiple birth, but these are the exceptions. As long as the shepherd is alert, his flock adequately housed and well fed during the five-month gestation period, and confidence and calm pervade the barn, there should be little trouble.

One of the first signs that lambing is near is the enlargement of the ewe's udder. When birth is imminent, the vulva will become swollen and red, and the ewe will seek solitude and be restless, circling and pawing the bedding. If the barn is crowded, now is the time to confine her to a lambing pen—a portable 4′ x 4′ hinged wooden fence which provides privacy and restricts her movements. Once the ewe is in labor, she should produce her lamb quickly. If labor continues for an hour, the shepherd should investigate the cause of delay. Difficult positioning can occur in the ewe's womb, as it sometimes does in humans, and the shepherd will have to realign the lamb for normal delivery and/or actually help deliver it. Once it has been dropped, the lamb's nostrils are cleared, and it is encouraged to nurse until the mother takes over. Rarely will lambs be orphaned or unclaimed in the small flock.

It is also rare that a healthy animal is sterile. Ewes will come into heat with the coming of cold nights in the fall. Some breeds can be bred more than once a year. Separating the ram from the breeding flock in late summer and reintroducing him to allow him to run with the ewes for about 4 to 6 weeks in the fall, has the advantage of more closely regulating the lambing period (5 months minus 5 days later). In commercial flocks, early lambing is essential so the crop can be ready for the Easter market. However, on the small homestead, lambing is often more convenient if timed for the first balmy days of spring, when both the newborn and the shepherd will be more comfortable during late-night vigils.

Housing for sheep can be inexpensive and primitive even in the north. All that is required is a shelter that is dry, well-drained, free from drafts, and has a southern exposure. Packed dirt floors are excellent.

The biggest expense comes in feeding. Two acres of pasture will provide enough summer forage for from three to eight sheep. When this goes, they must be fed hay. A daily ration of 3 to 4 pounds per sheep should be enough. Putting out more hay than they can consume will encourage the sheep to scatter and waste it. Many shepherds grain their sheep before breeding them, at a rate of 1/2 to 3/4 pound per sheep a day. This is essential for the ram as well. Others grain sheep throughout the winter or leave off and begin again about a month before the lambs are expected, working up to about 1 pound a day. A properly fed animal will produce healthy lambs.

Because of either lack of land or the cost of fencing, some flock owners confine their sheep to the shelter and a small exercise yard throughout the year, but daily feeding is costly, and this practice is as confining to the homesteader as it is to the sheep.

The threat of wandering dogs is the shepherd's biggest worry. Although he usually can be reimbursed by the town for any losses dogs may cause, this is small recompense for the decimation of his flock. Electric fences, hedgerows, and combinations of stone walls and barbed wire have all been tried to keep sheep in and dogs out, with limited success. Woven wire fence about 36″ high, topped by a double strand of barbed wire, is recommended.

13

This fine flock of Cheviot sheep, a hardy meat-and-wool breed from the Scottish Border, was raised in Maine. Stephen T. Whitney photo.

Consider your basic reason for deciding to keep sheep, and select the breed (pure-blooded or grade) that will most nearly meet your needs.

Although from the earliest times sheep were sacrificial animals offered to appease the gods—then promptly consumed by the worshipers—their ancestors were prob-

ably more like goats and were kept primarily for their wool. These small, rangy creatures underwent intensive crossbreeding to increase the quality of both wool and meat. This procedure was most successful in the British Isles, where it formed the basis of much of Britain's wealth in the 16th and 17th centuries. In Spain, at one point, exportation of the native Merino, a sheep of unusually fine wool, was a capital offense. Merino crosses, especially from Australia and New Zealand, still provide some of the highest quality wool to be found.

For several centuries sheep have been considered dual-purpose animals, good for both meat and wool. Breeds have been developed that produce a good quality of both. The homesteader interested in keeping sheep is advised to spend some time reading, and talking to shepherds. Then he can make comparisons and select one or more breeds on his own.

If anyone in the farm family is interested in 4-H Club work, a small flock of registered sheep can be the basis of a good breeding stock to be shown at agricultural fairs. The sale of registered stock later on can help defray the costs of education.

For the common homestead operation, grade flocks will produce ample supplies of both meat and wool. Registration papers do not appear on the table with the lamb chops, nor do they help you in knitting a home-grown sweater.

Meat on the table at little cost is one of the advantages countrymen have. Spring lambs can be pastured all summer, cost-free, and slaughtered when they are from 6 to 10 months old. Ram lambs go to the slaughterhouse first, for only one male is needed to breed the farm flock. Depending on the breed and age, spring lambs will return from 35 to 60 pounds of dressed meat for your freezer. You can butcher them at home. Expect to get two legs of lamb, shanks, shoulder roasts, rib

and loin chops, as well as a good supply of stew meat. Or you can sacrifice some cuts for combinations that could include crown rib roasts, loin roasts, and a saddle of lamb.

Mutton has never been popular fare in this country. But elderly sheep (a ewe has a useful breeding life of up to 10 years) can be slaughtered to provide a good supply of stronger-tasting meat.

Aside from the meat supply, the farm flock will produce wool each spring. There is an increasing interest in wool, as in all things natural today. You'll find that a wide variety of spun, knitted, and woven materials can be made at home.

Shearing a sheep would be easy if it were possible to immobilize the animal for a good long period of time (it isn't). You can shear with hand clippers or electric shearers. Or you can hire a professional (at about $2.00 a sheep) to save frustration and get the job done quickly. The wool should be clipped so as to come off like a blanket—all of a piece; this makes it easier to sort, wash, and process for use. The more second cuts (corrections of previous mistakes) that have to be made, the less useful the wool. The staple should remain intact.

Sheep are usually sheared once a year. (If left alone, they will eventually shed their coats in bits and pieces, which may be useful as garden mulch, or stolen by some birds to line their nests, but will not benefit the homesteader.) Some professional shepherds shear just before lambing time in order to check the progress of the ewes and help the lambs to find their mothers and

15

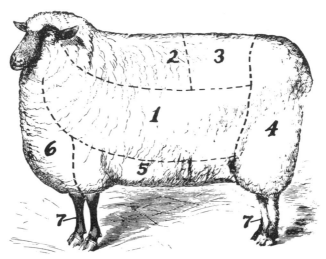

Wool chart: the numbers 1 through 7 indicate the areas from which the best (1) through the worst (7) grades of wool are obtained.

nurse more easily. Shearing after lambing, provided the shepherd has done some hand clipping around the udder and tail, will keep the ewe warm if the weather turns cold again, and will be less disturbing to the ewe at a time when she needs peace and reassurance.

As a natural resource, wool has countless uses. Homespun wool can be made into an article of clothing, worn, washed, darned, and then—when other material would be discarded—cut into strips and used to make newer, larger, or more stylish articles.

If crafts such as spinning, weaving, and knitting figure in your reasons for keeping sheep—as they should—you will first have to learn to wash and card. Washing raw wool can be a tedious process. Some craftsmen prefer to spin the fleece after it has been trimmed and wash it in skein form. Wool with its natural lanolin is easier to handle at the wheel. Teasing and carding are steps to take before the wool is spun. This involves pulling apart the fibers and aligning them so a continuous thread can be spun.

Wool fibers each have tiny scales which help them cling together and trap air and give them an insulating effect. Spinning is the process by which the fibers are twisted upon themselves in varying thicknesses, depending upon the nature of the fleece and the skill of the spinster. This can be done with a drop spindle, as it has been done for centuries, or on a wheel. The latter goes faster. Beware of buying an antique wheel unless it is in perfect condition or can be made so without great expense. They are likely to be

Meat chart: 1— loin; 2— leg;
3—ribs; 4— shoulder; 5/5— breast.

either missing vital parts or so worn and warped as to be useless. Better to investigate modern spinning wheels. There are many on the market that you can assemble yourself.

Knitting home-grown sweaters, hats, mittens, and socks to keep the weather at bay may not occupy all your time or talent. The next step is to learn to weave. On the loom you can make mats, clothing, blankets, rugs, upholstery, and drapery material.

There are still woolen mills in New England which will take your wool clip and convert it to washed, carded, and spun wool in various plies. This process will reduce your raw wool by approximately one-half. If your flock produces more than you can possibly use, sell the excess at the regional wool pool, or save it for craftsmen whose location or zoning prohibit them from keeping their own sheep.

With proper management, sheep pay many dividends—even a small flock. If you love working with animals, and can develop the taste and skill for homecrafted products, sheep may well be a project worth investigating. And even if there were no other justification for keeping sheep, the frolics of spring lambs on a greening pasture make it all worthwhile.

References
Teller, Walter M. *Starting Right with Sheep*, Garden Way, Charlotte, Vt., 1973.
Kluger, Marilyn *The Joy of Spinning*, Simon and Schuster, N.Y. 1971.

Digging and Stoning a Well

STONEMASONRY IS A DYING ART. So is well digging. To find a capable countryman who can both dig a well and stone it up is nearly a fruitless quest. Labor costs and newer methods of finding water have limited the appeal of this ancient profession.

But the homesteader—as interested today as he ever was in locating a dependable source of water for his house and barns—can dig and stone his own shallow well if he labors for love and experience. And if he lives in hilly country, he can also pipe the water to the house by gravity and keep both costs and maintenance to a minimum.

The first settlers were drawn to natural springs. These were later enlarged and stoned and sheltered to keep perishable foods longer and to provide a haven of coolness on a sultry summer's day.

It is possible to resurrect a dug well of proven ability. Or the homesteader can dig and stone one himself. Drilling wells is less risky today than it was even 20 years ago because of advances in technique and equipment, but it is still a gamble and often an expensive business. While it is true that shallow dug wells may dry out in extended periods of drought, they will provide an energyless source of water when operating.

Shallow wells are cylindrical holes usually about 3 feet in diameter and from 4 to 25 feet deep. Anything beyond this depth is termed a deep well; anything more than double the diameter is often called a cistern or reservoir. Although dug wells may be over 80 feet, these are rare.

Many shallow wells that were constructed 200 years ago here in New

England are still in operation, although with the increase in water consumption by the average American family (estimated at 350 gallons per day), they are often used to supplement a drilled well or as a stand-by source in case of power failure. Many are in their original shape, which attests to the art of the builder; others have been lined with protective sleeves or further deepened to increase the supply. Some were abandoned. They were either filled in with stone to prevent misfortune, or left planked over—a potentially dangerous practice as the plank cover rotted away.

Originally the dug well was covered with removable boards which allowed the water boy to sink his bucket and haul it up hand over hand or on a simple winch. Later the well sweep gained acceptance as a labor saver. Finally the pitcher pump was invented and mounted on planks or through a hole in a granite well stone, and the art of priming the pump and maintaining suction became progress. (The corollary art of challenging a little brother to put his tongue on a frosty pump handle was also developed about that time.)

One man who has considerable experience with dug wells is George A. Wood of Westminster, Vermont. According to a colleague, the retired Mr. Wood was never so happy as when diddling around in the bottom of a well—whether 8 or 80 feet down. He gained world-wide fame in 1967 on Valentine's Day when he was buried for six and a half hours in a 42-foot well that collapsed while being repaired. That February day, several concrete tile insertions slipped when Mr. Wood was installing them to shore up the sides of the well.

When Mr. Wood's helper shouted down that he was going for help, the veteran well digger is said to have called up, "Guess I'll be here when you get back."

A further cave-in buried him completely before help (in the form of a crane, three backhoes, an emergency rescue squad from Brattleboro, and television cameras) could get to him. For five hours he breathed through scuba diving hoses connected to oxygen tanks.

Digging or repairing a well can be dangerous, but not many homesteaders are going to dig too deeply. Most home wells in the country are from 6 to 15 feet deep. Once dug and stoned, a well should last practically indefinitely unless there is a marked change in the water table.

There are many bits of folklore and superstition to be investigated before starting to dig a well. One of these is dowsing, or water witching. Mr. Wood has no faith in dowsers—or rather, he has more faith in his own ability to judge from experience geologic formations, plant life, and the general lay of the land for aid in locating a projected well. He has pockmarked a considerable area on both sides of the Connecticut River valley with wells, never using a water witch.

There are those who claim dowsing is a gift possessed by only one in seven people. A research scientist recently announced that the art of finding water with a willow fork is connected with body chemistry and a peculiar alignment of neutrons and

19

protons inherent in the makeup of the dowser.

Despite the long-standing New England veneration of dowsing, Mr. Wood disdains it and has dug wells enough in his lifetime to prove that water can be found without it.

Once the site for a well has been selected, the homesteader can hire a backhoe which will dig down to 13 or 14 feet, or he can do the job laboriously with pick and shovel and buckets. A shallow well 3 feet in diameter will require an original excavation of more than twice that width. To dig a hole only 4 feet in diameter will hinder the digger; he needs all the space he can get to maneuver in.

Dug wells must penetrate to the ground-water table if they are to be sustaining. The water table generally follows the contours of the land and is higher under hills than beneath valleys. It may rise or drop during rainy spells and drought conditions. The bottom of the well must reach into the area of saturation.

Ground water travels for many miles. All water is constantly seeking its way to the sea, where it is drawn up again into the clouds to fall back on the earth in an endless cycle. Unless obvious sources of pollution are nearby (septic systems, livestock, open sewage, etc.), water will be purified as it moves through the earth. However, some water-borne diseases can travel for miles; others are attributable to faulty well construction, particularly where surface water penetrates the well. Some builders maintain that stones used in well construction must never

have been exposed to air as in that case they would already harbor forms of pollution.

All of this means that well water must be tested before it can be used for drinking. This can be done through your State Board of Health. Follow the directions for collecting water samples. The ensuing report will show with what chemicals and bacteria you have to contend. It will also recommend what to do to correct chemical imbalances, if possible.

Stoning a well is done without mortar. After the excavation has been made and a steady supply of water located, stones are laid in a circular pattern 3 to 4 feet in diameter. When a full circle is completed and chinked with smaller stones, the spaces outside the ring are filled with more stone to hold the well lining and provide an additional reservoir. Thus each circle is laid, chinked, and back filled. Mortar at this point would "seal" the source and increase the lime content in the well water.

The home well digger should consider the projected height of the well and estimate the amount of stonework necessary to complete the job. A short cut can be taken by investing in a steel culvert. This is held vertically by embedding stones and gravel around it and tamping in excavation dirt as the work progresses upwards. Or one could buy concrete well rings (3 feet in diameter, 2 feet high) and install them as he goes. Some well diggers prefer the latter, fearing that metal will eventually taint the water and increase the iron content.

No matter how deep the dug well, it must be protected from surface

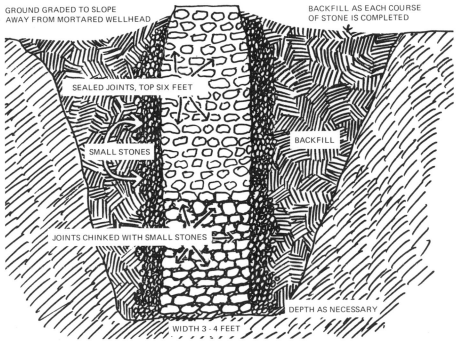

GROUND GRADED TO SLOPE
AWAY FROM MORTARED WELLHEAD

BACKFILL AS EACH COURSE
OF STONE IS COMPLETED

SEALED JOINTS, TOP SIX FEET

SMALL STONES

BACKFILL

JOINTS CHINKED WITH SMALL STONES

DEPTH AS NECESSARY

WIDTH 3 - 4 FEET

A stone well

contamination. The upper 6 feet of the well casing must be sealed on the outside with watertight cement grout (or good clay) and the exposed part of the well shaft mortared. The top should be capped with a man-hole cover or cement lid. Dirt can be mounded around the well head and sloped away from it, or trenches dug to prevent surface run-off from penetrating the shaft.

Removing the dirt while digging the shaft is a hard enough job. This can be done by the bucketload or by rigging up cables and pulleys to ease the load when the going gets deeper. Getting rid of the water is even more of a challenge once it starts seeping into the well site. A hose can often siphon the water off if the well is on a hillside. Otherwise, a gasoline-operated pump will be necessary if bailing out the well by buckets will not do the job fast enough. (One precaution *must* be taken when using an engine, however. Be sure to locate it as far from the well as possible to prevent the exhaust from entering the hole where you are working.)

To set up a gravity-feed water system (see page 22), the well should be

21

located at a level at least 50 feet higher than the house—the higher the better. One-half pound of pressure is assured for each foot of drop. Twenty-five pounds can be had with this minimum elevation. The delivery pipe must be buried below frost line in as straight and gradually sloping a line as possible. A stand pipe should be located in the well to allow accumulating air bubbles to escape or one may be tapped into the delivery line. A ram will be needed to boost the water from the well to a storage tank if the flow cannot be maintained otherwise.* The well outlet pipe should be covered with a strainer and located a foot above the floor of the well to prevent sand and dirt from entering the system.

While many authorities recommend lining the well floor with pea stone, Mr. Wood is opposed. He

*A hydraulic ram was once a common device. This helped to increase the velocity of the water by incorporating an air chamber and two valves between the source pipe and the drive pipe. For more information about rams, write: The Rife Hydraulic Engine Manufacturing Co., Box 367, Millburn, N.J. 07041.

suggests that any jagged surface such as crushed gravel will encourage snails and other forms of aquatic life to breed. (If one does find snails abundant in his well, he should dig down 2 feet around the well head, sprinkle a 70% chlorine solution in the trench, then pack good clay in the stone crevices before refilling the trench and grading the earth.)

Another country custom is to put a fish in the well to devour insects. If the well is properly sealed, Mr. Wood contends that you will not have enough insects to bother about. You *will* have a dead fish to scoop out. There are many kinds of pollution to contend with; no need to add obvious ones.

Few old-time stone wells need repair except in the upper several feet, which should be checked and remortared periodically to prevent surface water and wildlife from entering. If, however, a dependable well shows signs of deterioration, it can be shored up by telescoping round sections of steel tile in the shaft. The top section, for example, might be

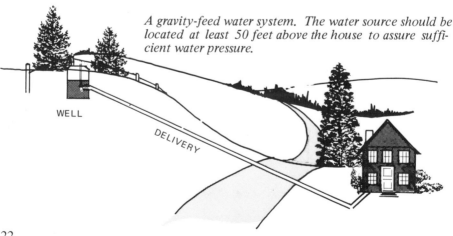

A gravity-feed water system. The water source should be located at least 50 feet above the house to assure sufficient water pressure.

WELL

DELIVERY

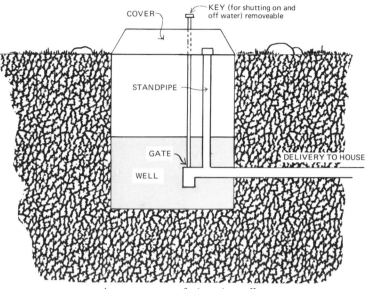

Arrangement of pipes in well

4-feet in diameter. This is inserted in the well to a stopping place. Another collar 3-1/2 feet is lowered inside and below the first, etc. Finally all sections are grouted to prevent seepage.

Ancient dug wells may be encouraged to produce more water by driving a specially constructed head with a perforated section below the well floor. This is pounded with mallets or weights and sections of pipe added until the water supply is markedly increased.

Although accustomed to working underground in cramped quarters with constant exposure to all kinds of possible danger, Mr. Wood remains remarkably calm. In his opinion the greatest drawback to his career in well digging and repairing is not the danger—which he tends to minimize—but the stench of a dead and disintegrating snake which from time to time he has been summoned to bucket out from someone's well. It's worse than a woodchuck or a skunk, he claims, and certainly far worse than being buried alive and living to tell about it.

References
Farmers' Bulletin 2237 USDA: *Water Supply Sources for the Farmstead and Rural Home* (Available from the U.S. Government Printing Office, Washington, D.C. 20402—price 15¢).
Kains, M. G. *Five Acres and Independence*, Pocket Books, 1948.

How to Build a Smokehouse

Smoking meat is usually a midwinter chore, but summer is the time to plan your smokehouse, while the weather still holds and your pig is gaining weight. It can be a simple, open-ended barrel, a permanent stone or cement-block outbuilding, or any number of variations in between.

Smoking heightens the flavor and color of pork. It also helps seal the pores to guard against deterioration by mold and insects, solidifies the meat for long-term storage, and increases its keeping power.

The earliest settlers smoked their meats under primitive conditions. Once they were established, they incorporated a smoke hole in the chimney construction of their houses. This was a bricked or stoned closet—with access from the back side of the chimney or from the second floor—through which smoke passed on its way up the flue. Meat was suspended from hooks and direct heat from the fireplace was deflected. Too much heat during the smoking process is detrimental to the finished product; high temperatures will cook the fat and allow smoke to penetrate too quickly, making the meat strong-tasting and stringy.

If your house is not equipped with a smoke hole—or if to use it would be hazardous—you can build a makeshift barrel smokehouse outdoors, make a portable wooden shelter that can be stored away, or construct a permanent building.

The easiest arrangement to set up is the barrel. Some countrymen merely knocked out both ends of a wooden barrel, set a smudge of corncobs within it on the ground, suspended their hams and flitches of

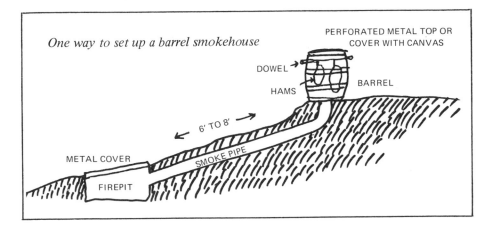

One way to set up a barrel smokehouse

PERFORATED METAL TOP OR COVER WITH CANVAS

DOWEL

HAMS

BARREL

6' TO 8'

METAL COVER

SMOKE PIPE

FIREPIT

bacon from dowels at the barrel head, and covered it all with canvas or other heavy material to keep the smoke from leaking. The disadvantages of this method are that only a little meat can be smoked at one time, and it is inconvenient to keep the smudge going continuously.

A more permanent barrel method is to bury a six-inch-diameter ceramic tile pipe sloping upwards from a fire pit to the smoking barrel. This pipe should be 6 to 8 feet long. Composition sewage pipes will not stand up to the heat and therefore tend to burn should your smudge get too hot. The resulting odor of creosote will permeate your hams and bacon and thereby ruin them. The ceramic tile pipe will conduct the smoke but discourage too much heat. The fire pit cover, which helps regulate the draft, must be metal to prevent it from charring or burning through. A metal disk can be suspended above the pipe where it enters the barrel to spread the smoke and prevent drippings from running

down the pipe. Meat is hung from dowels in the barrel head.

For those who have both room for storage and a larger amount of meat to smoke, the portable wooden smokehouse is an easily built structure. Tongue-and-groove boards are used to prevent leakage. Because the building is held together with only eight screws, the sides and roof can be knocked apart and put away for another year. The fire is made in a metal bucket at the bottom of the smokehouse and can be tended by reaching through the lower door. For safety, the firepot should be set on cleared ground or on a large flat stone. Meat can be hung from moveable 2" x 2" rafters and checked by opening the upper door. Air vents in the gable ends of the building regulate the draft and passage of smoke.

By far the most permanent smokehouse is the kind built and operated by Charles Fox of Canterbury, New Hampshire. This is a mortared fieldstone outbuilding about 7' x

25

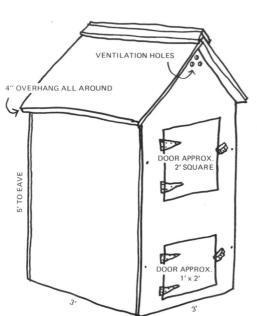

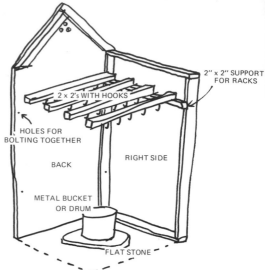

VENTILATION HOLES

4" OVERHANG ALL AROUND

5' TO EAVE

DOOR APPROX. 2' SQUARE

DOOR APPROX. 1' x 2'

3'

3'

2" x 2" SUPPORT FOR RACKS

2 x 2's WITH HOOKS

HOLES FOR BOLTING TOGETHER

BACK

RIGHT SIDE

METAL BUCKET OR DRUM

FLAT STONE

Above: *Portable wooden smokehouse, bolted together and easily dismantled.* Below: *A well-constructed permanent smokehouse.*

9' with a cement floor, drain, and detached fire pit. The eaves are 8 feet from the ground. Smoke vents in the gable can be opened and closed.

Fox is now a custom curer and smoker, licensed by the state, but when he built his smokehouse he was only interested in home production. Soon he was smoking hams for his neighbors. During eight months of commercial smoking— with additions to and changes in the original structure—Fox has processed 800 pigs. Most of them were brought, dressed, to his farm home.

The fire pit is located on the north side of the building and slightly lower, to allow smoke to enter through the smokehouse floor. (This is being changed, as Fox

If protected from insects and animals, smoked meat can be left hanging in a smokehouse which does not get too hot in late summer.

found that north winds in winter hindered fire-tending. The new fire pit will be on the opposite side.)

The smokehouse took all one summer to construct. Piles of stone were brought in before building began. A standard cement-sand mix of 1 to 4 was used. The first step was to erect forms to contain the the stones as the walls went up, but these were soon discarded to allow Fox and his family to see the results of what they were doing. Walls went up by eye, and work was slow. Fox tried to find stones that had at least two flat sides, a challenge even though his property abounds in stone walls.

Originally the interior was sheathed in plywood, but this was replaced by asbestos to comply with state regulations when Fox was granted a commercial license.

Fox uses red oak to smoke his bacons and hams. Traditionally, hickory is associated with smoked meats. "There isn't enough hickory in this area," he says. "Old-timers around here used red oak. It takes two years to dry, so if you use it the first year, you get more smoke than fire."

He pulled open the fire-pit door to show a couple of slightly glowing, split logs. "You don't need much wood," he explained, "to get the right amount of smoke."

Fox uses only corncobs to get the fire started. As with every art, each practitioner has his own methods and often disagrees with all the other experts. Apple wood and hard maple are other commonly used woods. Resinous woods must be avoided; they will taint the flavor.

27

Wood used green will produce more smoke than heat. If the fire burns too hot, throw on some hardwood sawdust to dampen it. Should you start your fire with pine, be sure the twigs or chips have burned out completely or have been removed before shutting the smokehouse door.

Cured meat absorbs smoke slowly, so do not fill the smokehouse with a thick cloud. It is better to let the smoke trickle among the hanging, separated cuts. Otherwise it can discolor rather than permeate the meat.

Some practitioners smoke continuously for two days; others start a smudge whenever they happen to be going by. This might take several weeks to achieve the proper color and flavor. Charles Fox smokes his hams four days continuously, keeping constant watch over the temperature.

For home production, your taste and schedule will determine the method to follow. Some must have their hams mahogany-color before they consider them processed.

Smoked meat can be left hanging in the smokehouse (provided it is safeguarded against insects and animals) if the building does not get too hot later in the summer. The meat can be brought into the kitchen when needed. Otherwise, it should be hung in a well-ventilated, dry, dark place. Some wrap their hams in cheesecloth and paper before hanging. Mr. Fox suggests storing hams in loose-fitting plastic bags in the bottom of which is a crumpled sheet of newspaper to catch the drippings. The covering must be loose to allow air circulation, which discourages mold.

Smoking meat for home use need not be a rigorous occupation and is certainly not harassed by regulations. Because pork is the meat most commonly smoked on the farm, care should be taken to follow assiduously each step in the butchering, curing (see page 33), and smoking processes. Pork spoils quickly if allowed to remain too long under unfavorable conditions.

With so few meat processors left in the country, building and operating your own smokehouse may lead you to experiment with different kinds of meat and cheeses you had not thought possible to preserve at home.

Reference
Wigginton, Eliot, ed. *The Foxfire Book*, Anchor Books, Doubleday and Co., Inc., New York, 1972, pp. 199-201.

Coping with a Whole Pig

Of THE SEVERAL WAYS OF DEALING with a whole pig that has been slaughtered and is ready to prepare, the easiest and most dramatic is to serve it young for Christmas dinner, decked out with holiday trimmings. Roast suckling pig is a special treat that predates the omnipresent turkey and even the traditional goose.

A pig on a platter is easy to handle. However, if it has outgrown the oven by several hundred pounds and four or five feet at this time of year, it will require the efforts of more than one person to turn your assets into a home meat supply that will last part of a year. This can be done by getting a pork chart, assembling some elementary kitchen tools, and reserving a period of uninterrupted time.

If slaughtering anything poses a major problem, get an uninhibited countryman to do if for you. (The majority of providers we know would all be vegetarians if forced to kill their own meat—particularly if it is home grown and has a name.)

Preparing a Suckling Pig

At six weeks a suckling pig will weigh 12 to 15 pounds and serve eight people. To prepare a small pig for roasting, wash it thoroughly inside and out, giving particular attention to the ears, snout, and feet. Remove the eyes and place a block of wood between the jaws.

Now dry the pig with a clean towel and set it to one side while you concoct your dressing. There are a variety of ways to season and decorate a suckling pig, but because pork is naturally rich in fats, the dressing should not be fancy. Use about 1-1/2 loaves of white bread

29

(1-1/2 pounds bread crumbs) and mix a seasoned dressing as you would for poultry. One variation could include cooking 4 large sliced onions in 1/2 cup butter until tender and golden brown. Add this to the bread crumbs, along with peeled and grated apples, dried sage or savory, and salt and pepper to taste.

Loosely stuff the cavity of the pig until the pig appears naturally plump. Sew or skewer the opening. Place the pig on a large baking pan or roaster, with the front legs folded under and tied in a kneeling position. Add 1 cup cold water to the pan. (You can encase the ears and tail in foil to prevent scorching.) Season well with salt and rub or brush the pig liberally with melted butter or olive oil. Then cover the whole pig with buttered paper.

Bake in a moderately slow oven (325°) and baste frequently with drippings for 3-1/2 to 4 hours (25 to 30 minutes per pound), or until tender when tested with a fork. If by chance the skin becomes brittle during cooking, rub it with a clean cloth dipped in melted butter and replace the buttered paper with a fresh one, butter side down.

Remove the foil from the ears and tail during the last 1/2 hour of cooking. When done, place the roasted pig on a hot platter or cutting board, untie the legs and replace the wooden block with a polished red apple or half a lime or lemon. Insert cranberries, cherries or green grapes in the eye sockets and make a garland of parsley or mistletoe for the neck. Set off your pig with a bed of parsley or watercress. (Some insist that a browned and golden pig is enough by itself to whet the Christmas appetite and should not be decked out to look like a clown.) Make a thick gravy with some of the juices and serve separately.

There are two ways to present a suckling pig to your guests: (1) carve it in front of them, or (2) after they have been seated, circle the table with the platter and retire to the kitchen to carve in privacy. The confident carver (1) will begin by making incisions one inch apart at right angles to the backbone, then run the carving knife along the backbone and under the meat to loosen it. Or the novice (2) can cut off the head, slit down the back, take off the hams and shoulders, and separate the ribs to expose the dressing.

Butchering a Whole Pig

A full-grown pig raised on garden surplus and milk, or bought slaughtered and halved lengthwise in anticipation of a winter's meat supply, poses a different problem —one of greater proportions and more work. The reward of butchering a pig at home is that every scrap can be put to some use.

Slaughtering is traditionally done after cold weather arrives and continues—depending upon the family's needs and supply—until early spring. Although animals can be killed whenever they reach a profitable size regardless of the season, unless you have cooling facilities you had better follow custom because meat, especially pork, deteriorates rapidly when exposed to warm temperatures.

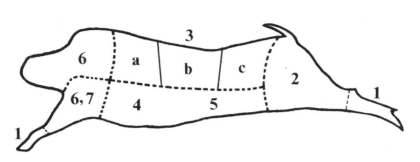

1) *Saw off fore and hind feet.*
2) *Ham—remove ham by sawing hip bone. Trim ham by removing tail bone, hip bone and slip joint.*
3) *Loin—one gigantic whole loin roast or: a) shoulder chops or shoulder roast; b) center cut chops, loin roast or crown roast; c) loin roast or sirloin pork roast, and pork tenderloin or loin chops. (Or Canadian bacon, under spine in cavity, but no roasts then.)*
4) *Spare ribs—saw between second and third ribs.*
5) *Bacon—cut off slabs.*
6) *Shoulder—saw for picnic and butt hams or for whole smoked or fresh shoulder.*
7) *Bacon—take from shoulder bone.*

To minimize waste, always keep a butcher's chart in view while working.

Therefore, hang the split carcass in a shed or garage only just long enough to allow the body heat to escape—24 hours at a temperature of 32° - 40° F. Then start immediately to cut it up. Cooling the carcass will firm the meat and make it more manageable. It will also give you time to assemble your tools and equipment and decide on what kinds of cuts will best suit your family's needs.

The tools you need for home butchering are simple. Have an array of sharp knives and a sharpener handy. Purchase a meat saw (about $5.00 at the local hardware store). Assemble a wooden mallet, meat grinder, butcher's twine and scissors, freezer paper and tape, and a sturdy cutting board.

If you are a purist when it comes to sausages, you will use as casings the pig's intestine, washed, stuffed and tied off in links. Otherwise, you will either have to buy sausage casing and a gun or make your own cloth bags from muslin (cylinders about 12″ long, 3″ in diameter). For curing hams, sides of bacon, and

31

layering salt pork, it is good to have an assortment of stoneware crocks of various sizes. If these are not available, use metal or plastic trash cans lined with two plastic garbage bags. If you are going to smoke your meat, you should already have taken this into consideration, but a smokehouse arrangement can be constructed (see page 24) while the meat cures in the brine.

When all of these considerations have been dealt with and the carcass has cooled, you are ready to move it into the kitchen and start.

There are several ways of approaching a 200- to 300-pound pig once half of it is laid out on the table. Procure a pork chart like the one a professional butcher uses and study the bone structure and possible cuts. Try to get someone with experience to look over your shoulder and offer suggestions as you proceed for the first time. (See the chart on page 31 for a cut-by-cut approach.)

Even a 200-pound pig (live weight) will provide you with approximately 55 pounds of hams and shoulder, 40 pounds of bacon and loin, and countless other benefits.

Tackle and finish half a pig at a time. Then you can either duplicate your efforts or vary some of the cuts—remedy your mistakes—when you approach the second half. Your initial attempts may not look like those under cellophane in the store downtown, but yearly practice and note-taking will show you how to improve.

Have two large pots ready on the stove to receive the fat which is to be rendered into lard. Remove the leaf lard first. This lies in flakes in the cavity of the pig's belly covering the loin and can be pulled out in layers. Cut it up and throw it into the pot. Leaf lard is the finest, whitest lard for pastries and can be stored in the refrigerator or sealed in canning jars and kept indefinitely on the pantry shelf.

The second pot is reserved for all the rest of the fat (including trimmings from the hams and shoulder) and makes lard for general cooking —or a supply of fat for making soap (see Book One, page 58).

As you butcher, divide the cuts of meat into piles depending on their final disposition: those that will be put in a brine or salted down (hams, shoulders, sides of bacon, salt pork, pig's feet); those used fresh or frozen (pork chops, roasts); and those to undergo further processing (sausage meats, head cheese, scrapple). If eating the internal organs (heart, liver, kidneys) does not appeal to you, refrigerate or freeze them, labeled, to provide meals for the dog and cat. Long before the "pigskin" was monopolized by school boys, the washed and inflated pig bladder was being kicked around by farm boys.

After butchering half the carcass, refrigerate what you have done and tackle the other half right away; otherwise, in the heat of the kitchen the meat will become as soft as butter and unworkable.

When all the cutting has been done and lard is simmering on the stove, trim, wrap, and tag meats that are to be frozen in order to clear space for what is to come.

Curing Hams and Bacons

When you have trimmed the hams and shoulders of excess fat, dry them off with a towel and weigh them on the bathroom scales. Then rub generously with kitchen salt and let stand overnight in a cold place. In the morning wipe dry and pack them into crocks or plastic containers—hams first, for these will take the longest time to cure, then shoulders, and finally the sides of bacon. Find a place in your cellar where they can remain cool during the curing process.

Now turn your attention to making a brine. One standard recipe suggests 8 pounds salt, 2 pounds brown sugar, 2 ounces saltpeter, and 4 to 6 gallons water for each 100 pounds of meat. Although there are many variations, this seems to be the maximum proportion of salt one should use. Pour in the brine to cover, and weight down the meat with a board or plate loaded with bricks or stones. Never allow metal to come in contact with the brine. To prevent spoilage while curing, the meat must be under the brine at all times. If the liquid evaporates appreciably, add more and stir. If it sours, mix a new brine.

Curing time varies according to the thickness of the meat and the amount of salt in the solution. With this brine it will take about 9 days to penetrate each inch of meat thickness. Therefore, sides of bacon will be cured before the larger pieces and should be taken out and stored in a cold place until everything is ready to smoke. Some inject brine into their hams close to the bone where the meat is most likely to spoil. This is done with a brine pump (like an oversized hypodermic needle) and will hasten the process. Thoroughly dry the meat before smoking (see page 28 for smoking procedure). Some people like to mix a paste of molasses and cracked pepper and rub it into the hams just before smoking.

Sausage

Good sausage is composed of about 25% fat. Meat scraps are put through a grinder, seasoned, and stuffed into cylindrical casings. Then they can be frozen. A good country recipe for breakfast sausage is: for 9 pounds of pork, mix in 2 tablespoons dried, rubbed sage or thyme, 1/4 cup salt, 2 tablespoons black pepper, and 1 teaspoon red pepper (optional).

Headcheese

This is a country delicacy much admired by some; for others, the preparation of the head is enough to kill future appetites. If your aim is to use all of the pig, you will have to face the head eventually. To make head cheese, remove the brains, eyes, and snout. Soak the head in cold water to rinse out the blood, then put it in a kettle of fresh water. (Throw in the tail. Not many cooks are ingenious enough to plan a menu around one pig's tail.) Bring to a boil and simmer until the meat falls from the bone. Discard the bone (save the broth for scrapple) and chop up the meat. Add enough liquid to cover, season with salt and pepper, add 1 tablespoon ground mixed herbs, like onion, garlic, and savory. Simmer for 1/2 hour longer. Pour into a loaf pan, cover with cheesecloth, and weight with a plate or board while chilling overnight. Unmold and slice to serve. (This may be kept frozen up to 3 months.)

You can also seek out recipes for scrapple (ground bits of cooked meat combined with broth from the headcheese and thickened with cornmeal), pig's feet, tongue, and ears if thrift and specialized taste govern your planning.

One by-product of the pig—and there is a lot of it if the animal has been well fed—essential to enhance the pots of baked beans featured in your winter menus is the meat-laced fat that will become salt pork. To prepare salt pork, cut chunks about 2″ x 4″ and rub generously with salt. Pack into a stoneware crock with a layer of salt between each layer of pork. You can dip into the crock from time to time all winter, but be sure that it is stored in a cool place and well protected from scavengers.

Reference
Wigginton, Eliot, ed. *The Foxfire Book,* Anchor Books, Doubleday and Co. Inc. New York, 1972, pp. 189-207.

Simple Wooden Toys That Last

Toys HAVE TRADITIONALLY BEEN made to imitate objects in the adult world. Their success depends on the outlook and skill of the toy maker and the kind of material he is using.

To make a wooden toy, all you need is a saw, a hammer, and a drill. Or you can rely on a sharp penknife and bring back the forgotten art of whittling. To assemble and finish your product, stock up on glue, sandpaper, and a can of boiled linseed oil (or non-toxic paint).

Of course, electrically-powered tools will make the job go more quickly. A band saw, jig saw, or saber saw are all useful. A hand-held electric drill into which you can also insert a hole-saw attachment, a shaper or sandpaper disc will likewise save time. All of these power tools are relatively inexpensive.

Begin with a home-crafted project which needs a minimum of supplies and equipment. Such a toy might be a climbing bear or a small log cabin.

The bear teaches coordination to the young. It is attached to the ceiling and can reach the top of its climb on parallel cords only if each of these is pulled alternately. When the tension is released, the bear plummets floorward and is stopped by two dowels at the strings' end.

Here are the materials and plans necessary to make the bear (or cat, monkey, or whatever your creative spirit dictates):

A piece of 1″ pine board (with or without knots) 8″ x 7″—remember the actual measurement of 1″ milled board is 3/4″;

A 7″ x 1″ x 1/2″ piece from which the bear hangs (this

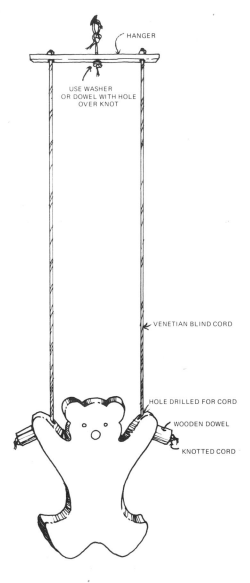

HANGER

USE WASHER
OR DOWEL WITH HOLE
OVER KNOT

VENETIAN BLIND CORD

HOLE DRILLED FOR CORD

WOODEN DOWEL

KNOTTED CORD

Climbing bear

could be gleaned from salvage if the grain runs lengthwise); 3 wooden dowels 1/2″ diameter x 3/4″ long, through which you drill a hole from top to bottom; 2 colored thumbtacks and 4 carpet tacks for mouth and eyes on each side of the board (or use a knot in the wood for the mouth and drill holes for eyes); About 10′ of Venetian blind cord.

Trace the pattern of the bear on your board, with the grain running vertically, using a piece of carbon paper. Cut around the outline. Drill a hole from the underside of the arm near each hand. Angle the drill about 45° so as just to miss the bear's ears if an imaginary line were extended above his head. Sand smooth and insert or drill the features.

Now drill three holes in the hanger (7″ x 1″ piece): one in the exact center through which a looped piece of cord will be inserted to hang it from the ceiling. Thread one of the dowels (or a washer) on the underside to keep the knot from slipping through. Drill the other two holes 1″ in from each end of the hanger. Cut the cord in half and insert one end through the hole and knot it. Do the same at the other end with the other piece of cord. Make sure these runner strings are knotted on the upper side of the hanger, for these will hang down to the bear; the central loop will extend upwards, with the knot and dowel underneath.

Thread the lower ends of the runner cords down through the holes in the bear's arms, then through the pieces of drilled dowelling, and finally knot them below the dowel to prevent the whole contraption from slipping to the floor.

Hang it from a ceiling hook and you have about as simple and durable a homemade toy as you can make. (A somewhat proficient 11-year-old boy could construct this for a younger brother or sister in about one hour.)

Try your hand too at whittling a toy log cabin with a hinged roof. You will need a saw, pliers, pen knife and glue, or a hammer and a supply of 1/2" wire brads. You will also need a supply of sticks about 1/2" in diameter for "logs," and a board scrap 5-1/2" x 3" x 1/2" thick for the floor.

Glue or nail two 5-1/2" logs along the front and back edges of the pine board so they become a log extension of the floor. Now notch each end of all subsequent logs as you work. Fasten two 4-1/2" logs across the ends of the floor so their notched ends are resting on the front and back logs. Proceed as you would in building a real cabin, alternating working on each side with the proper length logs (5-1/2" for the back, 4-1/2" for the sides). In the front, leave space to frame a door opening by using four 2" logs and anchoring them at the outside corners. To frame the opening and make it stable, split a log 1-3/4" long. Place these vertically, rounded sides inwards, and nail or glue them to the exposed ends of the four fronting logs.

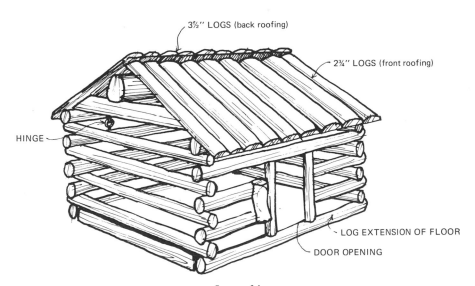

Log cabin

When your cabin is four logs high all around, it is time to construct hinges and raise the rafters.

The roof hinges at the back of the cabin. Hinges are made by drilling holes (about 1″ in from each end) down through two or more of the back logs, inserting a piece of heavy wire and bending over the top of each with pliers, to make loops.

Now for the roof. Three logs 5-1/2″ long are needed to form horizontal beams: one at the back into which you insert two small screw eyes and through these the loops of the already made hinges; one to rest on the front plate which extends above the door; and the third to form the ridge pole. Only two logs are needed for the gable ends. These will be 3-1/2″ long but angled at the ends so as to fit over the rafters and under the ridge pole. When

they have been fastened into position, split about five logs 3-1/2″ long and the same number of 2-3/4″ logs. These will be laid flat side down to form the roof. The longer ones are fastened to the back rafter at the lower end and to the ridge pole at the upper end; the shorter ones are fastened to the front rafter and their upper ends are whittled at an angle so as to tuck under the protruding ends of the back roofing.

When you have secured them and tested the roof hinges, you will have made a basic log cabin—a miniature mountain house that will inspire hours of play. If you have more time and material, embellish your cabin with a split log chimney (fixed horizontally to an upright wooden block) and a door on homemade wire hinges.

Try your hand at building a

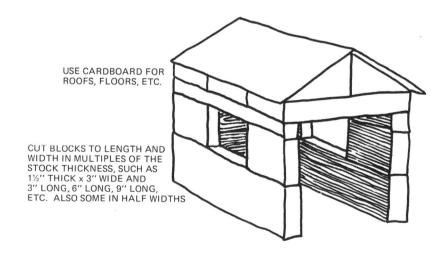

USE CARDBOARD FOR ROOFS, FLOORS, ETC.

CUT BLOCKS TO LENGTH AND WIDTH IN MULTIPLES OF THE STOCK THICKNESS, SUCH AS 1½″ THICK x 3″ WIDE AND 3″ LONG, 6″ LONG, 9″ LONG, ETC. ALSO SOME IN HALF WIDTHS

Other wooden toys easy to make from scrap material

larger structure like a barn or a doll house. Take the lead from home crafters of earlier times and you may soon be trying to imitate your surroundings in miniature. You may even tackle building a replica of the house you live in, all scaled down to a child's vision. Get a small one's help to plaster the walls, paint the trim, and construct a miniature brick hearth. After this, of course you will be urged to whittle replica furniture.

Wooden toys endure, and broken parts can easily be replaced at home from scraps of board.

Today's wooden toy makers are producing objects that take advantage of many of the properties of their material; its durability, solidity, and the beauty of grain and feel of wood.

"We're in the fantasy business,"

Shippen Swift says. He's president of Vermont Wooden Toy Company, Waitsfield. The more than 65 kinds of toys his company manufactures from native northern pine and maple are all wood and glue—good examples of the kind of indestructible toy that can be passed on from child to child and from generation to generation. No metal is used (even the wheels of rolling stock are pegged with wooden pins into wooden axles), nor is any paint applied.

Why not paint?

The junior partner and plant coordinator, Peter Rogers, quickly says, "Paint can cover a lot of mistakes. Making a toy of wood is still an artful job. Each part must be fitted and glued and sanded perfectly."

It also defeats the purpose of an all-wood toy. It covers the grain.

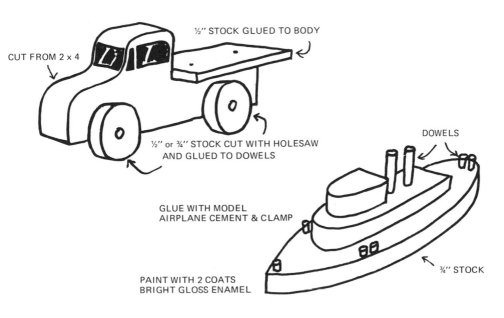

½" STOCK GLUED TO BODY

CUT FROM 2 x 4

½" or ¾" STOCK CUT WITH HOLESAW AND GLUED TO DOWELS

DOWELS

GLUE WITH MODEL AIRPLANE CEMENT & CLAMP

¾" STOCK

PAINT WITH 2 COATS BRIGHT GLOSS ENAMEL

"Paint adds to the cost, too," adds Donn Springer, an independent toy maker whose workshop is located in the Salmon Falls section of Rollinsford, New Hampshire. He is in his fifth year of producing wooden rolling stock—cars, trailer trucks, and imaginative push toys on wheels.

Springer rarely uses pine, which he maintains is too soft for rigorous use. Instead, he uses maple. This is a hard wood, and the oil finish he hand rubs on all his products brings out the beauty of the grain. He also uses birch veneer plywood from Scandinavia for the bodies of some of his trailer trucks.

For the axles and "hub caps" of his cars and trucks, Springer prefers metal—sometimes small metal rods with washers and caps, and sometimes pan-head sheet metal screws. He likes the action better than wooden dowel axles and pegged wheels and feels the metal hubs break the monotony of an all-wood appearance.

Most toy makers use white glue (either Elmer's or Franklin Tite-bond) to hold their products together. This will not color the wood and does not demand the exact temperatures required by liquid hide glue. But Springer points out he would use a water-repellent glue if planning to produce a toy boat.

"Wheels are the hardest thing to make at home," Springer says. The beginner might hit on the idea of sawing through a piece of suitable dowelling as he would slice a loaf of bread. "This leaves the grain running in the wrong direction and with any use at all, the wheel would eventually split right across its diameter."

A set of pine or hardwood blocks in various sizes and shapes is the basic fantasy toy and can easily be made at home. All you need is the wood, a saw, and some sandpaper. These allow children creative exercise of their imagination so important to their development. Blocks can be used to build houses and castles, caves and boats, or even labyrinths of secret tunnels and suddenly disappearing floors. True toys generate their own games.

Making Paint from Scratch

JUST BEFORE THE CIVIL WAR PAINT making shifted from the home to paint factories to supply the burgeoning needs of the urban population. Until then making paint had been the domain of the homesteader, itinerant painters and artists, and carriage makers. As reflected in William Dean Howells's novel of 1885, *The Rise of Silas Lapham*, fortunes were made and lost in early attempts to establish the paint industry.

Few people need to manufacture their own paint today, with commercial mixes available in a wide spectrum of colors. But for special projects, paints made in small batches at home can be economical, authentic, and the start of a challenging avocation.

One reason for reviving this forgotten craft is to obtain an authentic match to an existing color. Few commercial paints will do this. You may need the exact red of an antique bedstead to paint a rail replacement, a batch of yellow ochre to touch up scarred woodwork, or an old blue or green to piece out the side of a cabinet formerly built in. These are problems often encountered by people interested in restoring antique furniture and old houses.

All paint, essentially, consists of pigment (color) and a medium (the vehicle which carries the pigment and dries as a film to help protect the color from outside influences). To these two essentials can be added adhesives, dryers, thinners, varnishes, etc., depending on the kind of paint wanted and the surface to be coated.

Because countrymen were in the habit of using what they had or finding what they needed, they soon

41

discovered ways of bringing color into their lives by painting walls and woodwork, floors and furniture, houses and barns. They even took advice from the Indians who were said to be partial to combining salmon eggs and the bark from the red cedar. Linseed oil and turpentine were usually readily available; milk was on every farm. With combinations of these materials the homesteader either made paint himself or provided soured milk for the purpose to itinerant painters.

As the leading character in Howells's novel found, natural pigments abound in the countryside. Lapham discovered a fine deposit of earth oxides in the back pasture of his father's Vermont farm, and this led him to establish his paint works.

Local clays gave the reds, yellows, and grays so often found painted on early furniture and woodwork. Other natural dyes were used as well. These came from herbs, nuts, berries, tree barks—blacks from carbon, charcoal, and soot.

The combination of milk, pigment, and lime produced milk paint. Its tell-tale traces can still be found in the corners of antique furniture, around leg turnings and even soaked into the grain of wood unless some over-zealous refinisher has worn away the natural patina.

Milk paint is being marketed today by such men as Charles Thibeau of Groton, Massachusetts. As a lifelong lover of antiques and now as a maker of Pilgrim furniture and early wooden toys, he comes by his interest in paint manufacture naturally. By researching old recipes, garnering advice from chemist friends, and constant trial and error, Mr. Thibeau makes and fills mail orders for milk paints in the basement of his home.

"I deal in a specialized market," he says. "People who care for early furniture want it finished authentically. No modern paint will do this." He looks up from mixing one of his own products with a Mixmaster in the kitchen. In the next room his son is painting a reproduction hutch table that, according to the craftsman, will look like an original in 50 years. He quickly adds that to prevent future confusion each piece is branded with his mark.

Most early paints were much stronger-hued originally than they appear today after several centuries of use and abuse. Mr. Thibeau says that most of the pre-1750 furniture which we see in its "natural" state—refinished, rubbed, and polished to show the wood grain—was originally painted to take away the raw look and provide color as soon as the early settlers found the time or could afford the fashion.

Today Mr. Thibeau uses dry ingredients to make paint: powdered milk and pigments, lime, and probably several other essentials which he will not disclose. This solves the problem of packing, shipping, and ease of mixing and prevents spoilage.

Unless you have a basic knowledge of chemistry or can get the advice of experts, making paint at home is still largely a matter of trial and error. Few manufacturers will tell you their secrets. It is possible to find out the major ingredients but the proportions and the hidden additives which make theirs a distinguished product are closely guarded.

The Shakers, known for their colors as well as the design and construction of their furniture, often stained their products by mixing water with dry pigment, boiling it, and rubbing on while still hot. To get a smooth surface, they rubbed the wood later with pumice stone and wax.

Lime, pigment, and milk will produce a transparent color, often mistaken for a stain after several centuries of wear. The addition of whiting (Paris white and Spanish white are often mentioned in old recipes) helps make paint more opaque and gives it a better covering quality. This is *calcium carbonate*—limestone, shells, and tiny marine fossils—that has been washed and finely pulverized. The result of heating or calcining limestone is lime (*calcium oxide*), also called quicklime, burnt lime, and caustic lime. This was another principal ingredient of milk paints. Often old recipes will call for freshly slaked lime. This is *calcium oxide* to which water has been added. This step in home paint manufacture can be by-passed by purchasing hydrated lime (*calcium hydroxide*—lime that has already been slaked), which is the common agricultural lime.

Lime is an alkali or sweetener; soured milk is an acid. The chemical reaction of these ingredients is important in making a durable paint. They must neutralize each other, so that the combination is neither sweet nor sour. This can be tested in your kitchen by using litmus paper. The paper should not change color when wet with the lime-milk mixture. If the paper turns red, the mixture is too acid (add more lime); if it turns dark blue (too alkaline), add more soured milk.

You should be able to locate earth oxides in your neighborhood. Colored sediments and clay are often found in newly excavated ground, along roadsides and riverbanks, and in gravel pits. Dig them out and purify by adding water and boiling several times. Allow the sediment to form, filter out the impurities, and spread out to dry in a warm place. Then pulverize and store in airtight containers until ready to use.

For those who cannot dig them, dry pigments are stocked by a limited number of paint suppliers. They used to be part of the inventory of every country hardware store, but as ready-mixed and canned paints took over the market, the barrels of dry pigment once available were discarded and never re-ordered. The Johnson Paint Company, Newbury Street, Boston, Massachusetts, does still carry this kind of stock. There you will find umbers, ochres, siennas, Prussian blue, chrome yellows, Venetian red. Also available are pigments made from exotic imported woods and insects. Another supplier is the New England Resins and Pigments Corporation, Wakefield, Massachusetts.

Milk paints were used recently in recreating a stenciled room in one of the houses in Old Sturbridge Village. After experimentation with old recipes, the following combination was selected:

> Take a quantity of the curds of freshly skimmed milk [raw and soured]. To this add 1/5 of the volume of the above of freshly slaked lime. Mix together well to form a paste and then add 3 to 5 parts of water. To this now add a sufficient quantity of the desired dry color so that it is of a consistency that will run from the brush.

If a more opaque paint were wanted, another recipe was used, calling for 5 pounds whiting, 2 quarts skimmed milk, 2 ounces fresh slaked lime, and coloring to suit.

If you lack a source of raw milk, you can still duplicate an old-fashioned milk paint using commercial ingredients. To make a colonial red combine 1 quart buttermilk, 3/4 to 1 cup lime, 1/2 cup raw linseed oil, ground brick dust to suit, and Elmer's glue. The final ingredient, of course, is also a milk product and will give added adhesiveness and body. When applied to a new piece of wood, the paint produces a streaky covering that is properly old looking.

By combining skimmed milk and an oil, as in the following recipe, you can make an interior oil-water paint with good covering qualities:

> 1/ gallon skimmed milk
> 6 ounces lime
> 4 ounces raw linseed oil
> 3 pounds Spanish whiting (calcium carbonate)
> dry pigment to suit

Besides paint for their furniture and woodwork, countrymen also needed a dependable whitewash to spruce up plastered ceilings and lighten interiors of farm buildings. A recipe book of the past century provides the following "Government Whitewash." It is said to have been used effectively on the east end of the White House for years. You may want to try it:

> Take 1/2 bushel of unslaked lime, slake it with boiling water, cover during the process to keep in the steam; strain the liquid through a sieve or fine strainer, and add to it a peck of common salt previously dissolved in warm water; add 3 pounds of ground rice; boil to a thin paste and stir in while hot; add 1/2 pound Spanish whiting and 1 pound clean glue previously dissolved by soaking in cold water; add 5 gallons of hot water to the mixture, stir well and let stand a few days, covered from dirt. It should be applied hot for which purpose it can be kept in a kettle on a portable heater.

References
Andrews *Shaker Furniture*, Dover Publications
Gould, Mary Earle, *Early American Woodenware*, Chas. Tuttle, Rutland, Vt.
Mayer, Ralph *The Artist's Handbook*, Viking Press

Decorating a Wall with Old-Fashioned Stenciling

O NE WAY EARLY SETTLERS HAD OF sprucing up the homestead was to stencil a room with repeated geometric patterns in soft colors. This art form was born in the days of the new Republic, bloomed briefly, then perished when it was supplanted by a newer craze—wallpaper. Considered peculiar to New England and often practiced by itinerant craftsmen, wall stenciling had gained spotty acceptance as far west as Ohio and south to the Middle Atlantic states, before its golden age had run its course.

Today, interest in wall stenciling is undergoing a revival. For years art historians have recorded and photographed stenciled walls whenever news of one has reached them. Still, much of the work of the early stencilers has been lost, either through neglect or changing fashions. Now, with the pendulum swinging back to individual expression and simplicity, wall stenciling can fill a need because it can be practiced with very little equipment even by those who are not facile artists with a freehand brush.

One modern practitioner of this art is Ruth Wolf of Deering, New Hampshire, a professional stenciler of tinware and furniture, who was captivated by the stenciled walls she found in New England, many painted by wandering craftsmen in the early part of the 19th century.

One of the most famous of these craftsmen was Moses Eaton. His stencil kit—discovered in the attic of his house in Hancock, New Hampshire, and now the property of the Society for the Preservation of New England Antiquities in Boston—tells more about the man's

45

techniques than about the man himself. In it are the round, flat-ended stencil brushes he used, dry pigments, and a collection of original stencils he cut, many with the paint still adhering to their surfaces. Comparing these designs with finished walls, it is possible to speculate about both Eaton's work habits and his wandering.

Because few itinerant stencilers signed their work, it is difficult to establish the authenticity of a particular wall. Some stencils were undoubtedly copies by less adept craftsmen; artists may well have exchanged original designs.

Ruth Wolf has spent years tracing and reproducing authentic walls. Today her house, Hayfields,* is decorated with striking patterns, many of which she has reproduced from Moses Eaton's original designs. She has also stenciled the walls of other buildings in diverse parts of New England. One was the White Church in Grafton, Vermont, where from a scaffolding near the ceiling, she restored stencils while the building was being renovated; another was a house newly constructed on Nantucket, which the owners designed as a showplace for their antiques.

The stencil is essentially a mechanical device which allows the reproduction of a pattern over and over and assures more consistency than freehand design. Paint is applied through the cut-outs in the stencil onto the surface beneath. It is the same process packers use today to label boxes and crates.

*See *Yankee* Magazine, Oct. 1968, p. 134.

Unlike the freehand work of the fresco painter, where paint is applied to a wet plaster surface, wall stencils are executed on finished, dry areas of plaster or wood.

Mrs. Wolf was first taken with the simplicity and boldness of stenciled walls. Her years of training as assistant to Esther Stevens Brazer, founder of the Brazer Guild, which encourages the study and practice of stenciling in all its forms, helped her to see many of the problems of stenciling and to master the techniques. As a modern stenciler, she has devised her own methods of dealing with the art. Instead of using stencils made from varnished paper, leather, or tin, the way the early artisans did, she cuts hers from architect's linen. Rather than manufacturing milk paint (see page 41), she buys japan paints which she mixes with alcohol as a medium. A further refinement has been to discard the stubby brushes and substitute squares of velour, which she wraps around her index finger to apply paint through the cut-outs.

To decorate your walls in this way, you will require only a few items which can be bought at an art supply store: architect's linen, a stencil knife, japan paints in various colors, and alcohol. In addition, you will need some measuring devices: rulers, a plumb line or level to establish verticals, and possibly a chalk line.

Most important, you need a blank wall and some idea of how to decorate it.

Finding motifs or patterns to reproduce on your wall will be a challenge. You can trace them from existing walls with tracing paper and transfer the designs to architect's linen before you cut them out. Or you might want to investigate museum collections of stencils. Often organizations such as the Society for the Preservation of New England Antiquities or the State Historical Society in Concord, New Hampshire, will allow you to trace original stencils or have duplicates made. Or, you can design your room around personal themes.

No matter how you decide to lay out your design, you must first prepare a clean wall surface. If wallpaper has been removed, get all the paste off the wall. Often you will have to touch up cracks or blemishes if the plaster is old. Stenciling can be done on plasterboard or composition walls if you first give them several coats of oil base paint. If you wish your designs to appear on a tinted rather than a white background, now is the time to paint the walls a color complementary to the woodwork.

In the stenciling technique developed by Ruth Wolf, the design is first traced or drawn on architect's linen, then cut out with a sharp knife such as an X-acto.

With the stencil taped in position, the base color paint is applied with a forefinger wrapped in velour.

The second color or element of a composite design is applied after the first has dried.

The earliest stenciled walls (late 1700s) probably were only border designs that complemented the architectural detail of the room by outlining the woodwork. If the overmantle was plastered rather than paneled or sheathed, special attention was given it as the focal point of the room. Often early stencilers designed vases of flowers, weeping willows, paired birds, or, more rarely, the spread eagle, symbol of the young nation. Later, probably in the first decade of the 19th century, an overall stencil pattern was developed to imitate more closely the imported French wallpapers that were beyond the reach of all but the wealthiest.

Moses Eaton was distinguished for his division of space and use of color. Combinations of soft olive green and brick red marked his work. Often he introduced dark blues, black, and various shades of both pink and yellow to produce decorative patterns.

To divide the space, Eaton commonly stenciled a wide frieze of repeated patterns around the top of the room at ceiling height. He used a baseboard border (or sub-base if wainscoting was present) of a different design. The space between was divided into vertical panels by stenciled uprights. Finally, he decorated each panel with alternating motifs or units, some simple and others composite. A composite stencil is one for which two or more stencils have been overlaid to form a single motif. Each stencil introduces a new color and element to the basic design.

Ruth Wolf uses a sharp stencil

The finished wall – a reproduction of a Moses Eaton design.

knife to make the cut-outs. She places the linen on a square of glass, and with one hand cuts the design while the other is free to rotate the stencil when curves are needed. She is also careful to leave a large margin around each stencil which will help protect the wall while paint is applied. She marks or notches the top and bottom of each stencil so she can align them accurately.

Once a sufficient number of stencils have been cut, you are ready to begin decorating the wall. Lay out the frieze first; then the baseboard stencil.

To apply the paint, Ruth Wolf first dips her velour-covered index finger into a container of alcohol, then into japan color, and finally

Recently uncovered in a Hillsborough Center, N.H. home, this wall stenciling is thought to be the original work of Moses Eaton.

pats it onto the stencil. Only experience has taught her the proper working consistency of the thinned paint. If it is too thick, the application will be lumpy; if too runny, paint will escape under the surface of the stencil and will have to be corrected. (Let it dry before repainting the background with a freehand brush.) In her method she establishes an immediate contact with the stencil and wall and can control the final results better than with a stencil brush.

"There is a higher concentration of paint where you first touch the wall, less as the paint is used up and before you redip it in the paint pot," she points out.

She prefers this somewhat mottled effect since it softens the motifs and makes them appear more authentic, as though time had already made its mark. Composite stencils are done in stages. The first color is allowed to dry before a second stencil is laid on top of it.

Make sure to clean the backs of the stencils after each motif has been used. Otherwise, you will have to spend time retouching the smudges.

After the job is done, store stencils flat for future reference. Do not varnish or otherwise seal the finished wall. Time will soften the designs and make them look old.

The choice of stencil designs in early days was probably based on personal preference. Although little has been written about the meanings of the motifs, a few have special appeal. The famous pineapple design used by Moses Eaton and copied by others stood for hospitality and often appeared in homes as well as public rooms of taverns. Bows and hearts in the design of a bedroom welcomed a new bride.

While these were often combined with a bell, this motif was also associated with the founding of the new Republic and has been found in many tavern ballrooms. The weeping willow, often prominent in the overmantle design, stood for immortality.

The art of wall stenciling was doomed, except in isolated pockets where change was slow, when mass-produced wallpapers became available. Gradually artisans turned to other crafts; the stenciled wall became merely a quaint relic and was covered with more fashionable decoration.

Today several makers of wallpaper are marketing expensive copies of stenciled walls. The cycle has come around to imitating the imitation.

References

Little, Nina Fletcher, *American Decorative Wall Painting 1700-1850*, E. P. Dutton

Waring, Janet, *Early American Stencils on Walls and Furniture.* Wm. R. Scott, Inc.

How to Make an Apple-Picking Ladder

My long two-pointed ladder's sticking through a tree toward Heaven still. . . .

Robert Frost

IF YOUR WOODLOT CONTAINS A VA-riety of trees in different stages of growth and you have time to go beyond cutting cordwood this winter, there are many simple wooden products you can make to use around the farm and homestead. One of the most necessary is a ladder that will be light enough to carry around and yet durable enough to last for years.

There are craftsmen upcountry who supply dozens of ladders to professional apple pickers each year, but even if you are a rank beginner who can use hand tools, you can make a ladder from your own woodlot. Given certain basic tools on hand—a ripsaw, maul and wedges, mallet, drawknife or plane, hammer, pipe clamp, and brace with two different-sized bits—the only purchase you will have to make is a handful of 1-1/2″ (4d) finishing nails.

Once your wood has been selected, cut, dried, and shaped to specifications, it should take about an hour to assemble a safe, good-looking ladder.

Plan ahead to have the wood ready to use. Red oak makes good rungs. It is strong and durable yet can be worked while still green. It is easier to split and shave than white oak. For the rails use spruce or ash. These woods are relatively free from knots (which weaken a ladder), yet are light enough to carry in ladder form.

Select a tree for the rails from a thick stand in your woodlot. This will assure good, straight growth. To make a standard 18-foot apple-picking ladder (for which you will find many other uses), choose a tree that is about 4 inches in diameter at a height several feet off the ground. When you have felled it (cut to slightly more than your finished length) and brought it home, peel off the bark and trim all branches flush to the trunk with an ax.

The pole is now ready for you to rip it in half lengthwise and start the drying process. You can either rip tediously with a hand ripsaw or use a chain saw or bench saw. The last two of course will do the job much more quickly, but you will need plenty of room to maneuver and a helper to guide the saw. In colonial times, pit saws were used—one sawyer located on the super-structure above the log, and the other in the pit below.

Spruce may twist and warp while drying so you will have to restrain it for from 6 to 9 weeks depending on the weather. Construct four uprights about 4 feet apart. Across each, nail a pair of braces not more than 2 feet long. Leave room between each pair to insert your halved rails (flat side down) and a wooden wedge to prevent twisting (see diagram).

Professional ladder makers often cut their stock in late spring after the garden has been planted if they plan to complete the assembly in time for apple picking. However, harvesting the rails is something you can do at any time of year when work is slack.

Oak for the rungs will take longer than the rails to air dry, but you should work it into shape while still green because it will be easier to split when freshly cut. After you have felled your tree, saw several sections of the log into chunks 2 feet

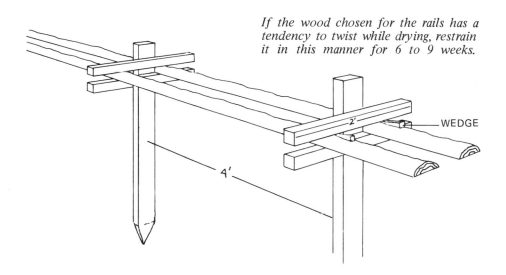

If the wood chosen for the rails has a tendency to twist while drying, restrain it in this manner for 6 to 9 weeks.

long. Now split these with your maul and wedges, quarter them, and reduce in size to 2″ x 2″ squares, 2 feet long.

A standard 18-foot ladder will require 17 graduated rungs, each decreasing 1/2 inch from a maximum length of 22 inches over all for the lowest rung. With a 4-inch tree, the inside measurement at the butt of the finished ladder will be about 18 inches. Dowel both ends of each rung to fit holes bored in the side rails. The first eleven rungs should be dowelled to fit 3/4-inch holes; the top six should be shaped to fit 5/8-inch holes. This helps prevent the upper reaches of the ladder rails from splitting.

The rungs themselves can be left roughly shaped for better purchase, or you may want to round them to avoid splinters while using the ladder. This can be done after the ladder has been assembled.

Use a lathe to dowel the ends of the rungs or clamp each in a bench vise and round them with a draw-knife.

When your material has been

When assembling the ladder, tap the rungs in one rail, flat side up, then place the last rail on the upright rungs and align from bottom to top.

After the first rail has been completely nailed, draw in the other rail tightly with either a pipe vise or clamp and nail the rungs into it.

properly cured, you are ready for the final step before assembling your ladder. Lay the pair of dry rails on the ground, making sure the butts are aligned. Mark off 1-foot intervals beginning from the bottom, and with brace and bit bore 3/4-inch holes, centered in the rails, to receive the first eleven rungs. Change to a 5/8-inch bit and bore the remaining six pairs of holes at the top of the ladder rails.

Now you are ready to assemble your woodlot product. Lay out your rungs in order of decreasing length,

the longest at the base of the rails and the shortest at the top. Set the rungs in one rail, flat side up.

Tap with a mallet or hammer until the rungs are properly seated in the holes. When you have completed one rail, place its mate on the upright rungs and align it from the bottom to the top of the ladder. Once each rung has been seated at both ends, lay the ladder on the ground and secure all of the rungs through one rail with 1-1/2″ (4d) finishing nails. This will keep the taper from pulling apart during use.

To prevent possible accidents or injuries to the user's hands, set all the nails, and saw off any excess tenons before the ladder is completed.

Once assembled, the ladder may be left to age naturally or rubbed with a coating of linseed oil to preserve the wood.

After the first rail has been completely nailed, draw in the other rail tightly with a pipe vise or clamp and nail the dowelled rungs in it. All nails should be set to prevent danger to the user's hands later.

Another safety measure to take before completing the ladder is to saw off any excess tenons and drawknife or plane rough spots and knots. You may even want to sandpaper the finished product to guarantee the user freedom from splinters as the rails guide him up and down the ladder. The wood can either be left to age naturally or rubbed with a coating of linseed oil to help preserve it.

Many apple-picking ladders are made so that the rails meet at the top to allow easier penetration of the upmost branches of the tree. However, if your ladder is to be used for several purposes around the farm in addition to harvesting apples— gutter cleaning, shingling, house scraping and painting—the tapered construction described will provide more stability than the triangular kind as you lean the top against a flat, ungiving surface.

Ladders made by expert craftsmen for professional apple pickers receive hard, seasonal use. Their life expectancy is between 5 and 7 years. However, the one you make and take care to keep dry should last nearly as long as you do.

PEACOCK

GUINEA HEN

PILGRIM GOOSE

Keeping Geese, Guinea Hens, and Peacocks

WITH INCREASING NOCTURNAL IN-vasions of rural areas by motorists, despite the energy crisis, some countrymen have arranged with the public service company to install street lamps to flood their dooryards with light while they sleep.

If you don't favor street lamps or a fierce watchdog but live far from neighbors, another way of alerting yourself to possible intrusion day or night is to keep geese, guinea hens or peacocks. These guardians will give the alarm at the slightest rustle of a wind-blown leaf or the approach of uninvited footsteps of man or beast. In addition, they will lend an exotic aura to your holdings and bring to your table luxuries usually reserved for festive occasions and to be had in this country only in sophisticated restaurants.

Each of these birds has been domesticated for thousands of years. Although guinea fowl are shorter-lived, geese and peafowl have been known to carry on from 20 to 35 years. So, if you choose either of the latter as night watchmen, expect a long-term relationship.

Geese

Geese have long been known in this country. The wild Canada geese honking in V-formation overhead foretold the coming of spring and the approach of winter long before colonists in New England were craning their necks skyward and speculating about the weather.

There are many varieties of domestic geese. Often fancied for meat and liver is the gray Toulouse. But Emden and African geese are also raised commercially here. The former was one of the first breeds imported; the latter has a distinctive knob at the top of its beak. Other kinds that are available include the brown and the white China geese, the Pilgrim and the Buff.

Whether geese are raised as guardians, meat-and-egg producers, or merely as farmyard pets, they demand little attention from their keeper. It is best to start a flock of geese by either purchasing a mature pair (from about $25 a pair) or buying half-a-dozen six-day-old goslings (about $1.50 apiece) and letting nature take its course. One course it will take is to tell you how many ganders and geese (males and females) you have bought, for it is difficult even among bird fanciers to be absolutely sure with goslings. Generally geese mate for life, but a single gander in a farm flock will be attentive to a harem.

Goslings grow rapidly. When you bring them home in late spring, they are merely fluffy balls with beaks and feet. Soon, however, they feather out, elongate, and come to fit their beaks. At first you will have to feed them *non-medicated** high-protein grain or mash, clabbered milk or bits of cheese, but as they and the season progress, 75% of what they consume will be in the form of green

*Medicated feeds or those with synthetic additives are poisonous to ducks and geese.

plants. Traditionally, flocks of geese have been set to weeding the strawberry patch. They can also keep down the weeds along the lanes and fence lines if they are started when the growth is low. They do not favor tall grass but prefer to work over areas already closely cropped.

When fall comes, feed them more grain (by then it can be daily pellets, sheep ration, or poultry feed); by Christmas a spring gosling will fill the holiday platter and weigh from 8 to 12 pounds dressed. Most cooks agree that anything more than six months old is a gastronomic disappointment. Certainly, beyond the age of two years they should be kept only as night watchmen, breeders or pets.

Once the gosling has developed feathers and a personality, he can generally take care of himself. Goslings need only some crude form of shelter during the winter, for they delight in waddling around in snow and sleet and keeping the waterhole free from ice. A pond is not necessary to keep them happy, even though they are waterfowl by nature. Water for drinking and preening is essential, though, and some countrymen insist it should be available in larger quantities during mating season.

The advantage of keeping only geese as night watchmen is that their gentle criticism of noteworthy but not catastrophic changes during the night will only take the form of guarded conversation. But let fear become an element, and they will take their jobs seriously and set up a honking and a hissing that can be heard a long way off.

Geese have the reputation of being vicious. They have been known to attack strangers and to bite. However, other than in mating season, when possessiveness blinds reason, geese raised from goslings will behave with respect and a certain broadminded awareness towards people they know. Besides, they come to like their feeder. They demonstrate a wary trust whenever he appears and will often continue to follow him around long after they are grown.

The greatest disadvantage in keeping geese, even given enough pasture for them to fertilize, is that they often prefer fertilizing the ground near the house, perhaps because it is off-limits, or because they need some human recognition of the job they have been assigned.

Guinea Hens

Guinea hens are another matter. These birds were first brought to Europe in the 16th century by Portuguese explorers from the west coast of Africa, hence their name. There they are still thought of primarily as meat birds, and although less abundant in this country, they are now achieving a sort of rural comeback.

A century ago it was a common sight to see a flock of guineas

A small flock of Pilgrim *geese, a breed unique in that the sexes differ in color. Adult males are white with blue eyes; females are grey and white with hazel eyes.*

59

roosting in the trees at night about New England farm buildings. They are wilder than geese, more flighty in their personality, and much funnier.

Guinea hens live only four or five years, but their short lifespan is made up for by their loud noise, the delicate gamey flavor of their meat, and their looks.

The most common varieties are the lavender, pearl, and white. Of these, the pearl—purplish-gray feathers with evenly distributed white spots—is the most common. The necks and heads are bare of feathers, often highly colored with red and white, and somewhat scaly-looking.

They reproduce once and sometimes twice a year. A pair of guinea fowl will produce from 12 to 20 offspring in a single hatch. Usually the female seeks the anonymity of a shrub in the middle of a meadow or along a fence line. You will not see her from late June through July unless you stumble across her nest. Miraculously she will appear one day in the barnyard followed by a cluster of quick-moving little balls of down. They are so fast in their apparently legless flight to stay within reach of their mother's protective wings that you will not be sure of your count until they have feathered out and slowed their pace.

Guineas will come to a familiar feeding place for a scattering of grain in the open barn at chore time, but essentially they are insect-eaters and prefer to wander. During the summer they roost in shade trees, take dust baths among the vegetables, stalk before the glass windows to admire their prehistoric looks, pick at pea blossoms and ripe tomatoes, and mince away in a bunch when reprimanded or swoop off in a flurry of angry wings. When alerted to danger, they will fill the air with high, piercing, monotonous, and slightly insane chants in unison, long after what they feared has passed.

These exotic birds will roost in the barn along with the bantam chickens in winter. Or they can be kept in captivity year-round, but like all wild birds caged, are prone to flighty pacing that makes chickens nervous; the guinea fowl will always be the first to raise the dust when you enter.

Peacocks

Peafowl and peacocks have never achieved real popularity among common farmfolk in New England. There is something so other-worldly about a peacock strutting on the lawn with an open fan that perhaps the Yankee's heritage prohibits him from accepting a fowl whose principal asset is beauty. These birds are sacred in their native India. They have been known for centuries in China and Japan and farther south in Java and the Malay Peninsula. They found their way west with travelers in pre-Biblical times to Egypt. It was the Romans who first served them on the table. It seems an enormous affectation to serve a roasted peacock on a platter—his fan extends five feet tall and ten feet across—for such a meager portion of meat. It is said, by those who thought to live on beauty, that peacock meat is a disappointment—

unpleasant, coarse and tough. For those who prefer exotic food rather than sustenance, perhaps a peacock served in full regalia is the ultimate answer.

For most who covet peacocks, it is enough to see them raise their fans and know their piercing voices will ward off marauders. You must live even farther out if you plan to keep both peacocks and your neighbors' tolerance. The cry for "help" a peacock raises when alarmed is so human it has led many rescuers on a fruitless search and driven off countless intruders as well.

Raising peacocks is a fussier business than raising geese or guinea hens, for the young must be taught to eat and drink if there is no peahen to show them how. One way to do this is to put colored marbles (the kind our children call "stickers" during spring recess at school) in the high-protein mash and water. The chicks will be attracted by the glint of these, peck at them, then somehow notice that food is attached to their beaks. They are also prone to blackhead, as turkeys are. This disease (carried by chickens) attacks their guts and will devastate both your flock and your investment. But if you get them off to a good start, your peacocks will be around for nearly 35 years, provided they escape predators and angry, sleepless neighbors.

Once grown, these semi-wild birds, closely related to pheasants, are more capable fliers than one would think. They will zoom over the barn at any threat and come to roost in trees.

There are many breeds of pea-cocks. The one most commonly seen is the blue and green variety. All of them prefer park-like surroundings to match their regal looks. They must have enough open space to show their plumage as well as ample shrubs and trees to flee to. The sight of a peacock in full regalia on the lawn is breath-taking. The tail feathers support the plumes of the male—each dotted with an eye according to the wishes of an ancient goddess. These are shed in late August but grow back again by April. During mating season, and even at the suggestion of admiration from a passerby, the male will spread his train and rattle it eerily to gain applause.

As their longevity suggests, peafowl are hardy birds. They mature in two years and the females begin laying in April. They can also be confined year-round rather than be left to strut upon the lawn and take their chances. For this you will need a large, wired enclosure some 15 feet square with a roost about 3-1/2 feet above the floor. This will allow the cocks to fan out without endangering their plumage. They should also be provided with a wire-enclosed sun porch. One male and two to five females do well together.

The cost of grain must be taken into account, for all semi-wild birds need a higher protein diet than chickens get. And keep in mind the ever-present threat of dogs and wild predators.

There are still enough raccoons and foxes, fisher cats, lynx and owls to decimate our flocks. Skunks make their nocturnal presence known by robbing nests of carefully tended eggs, and dogs range the countryside looking for mischief. Of course, all these birds can be reared in confinement, but half the pleasure in having them is in seeing them run free.

A final disadvantage may show up later. You may find yourself addicted to collecting exotic fowl. In this case, your facilities will increase, your risks multiply, and your finances dwindle. Some pairs of birds sell for more than $400.

Guinea hens and peacocks are game birds essentially and therefore present more of a challenge to prepare than chicken and geese. Because of their wilder habits, their meat is likely to be dry if roasted like a chicken, especially if the bird is getting on in age. (Breast of guinea hen is by far the choicest part of the bird; don't expect much from the legs.) Therefore, lard the bird with thin slices of bacon, salt pork, or larding pork if roasting. Cook until tender, about 20 minutes per pound. Often more satisfying results can be had by braising the bird. This is done by browning it all over in a skillet with a little oil and butter. Lift the bird out and set it aside while briefly cooking a couple of chopped onions and carrots in the skillet. Now place the vegetables in the bottom of the casserole, enter the bird, and add salt and pepper. Before covering, lay a piece of buttered brown paper over the bird to help keep in the juices. Cook until tender or for about 1 hour. To make gravy add about 1 cup soured cream to the casserole juices. Heat while stirring, but do not allow to boil.

Very little has been published about the care and feeding of guinea hens and peacocks. Learn about them from a local game-bird fancier; attend county fairs and write down the names and addresses of displayers. Follow your local market bulletin and the want ads in newspapers. Talk with your county agent.

Reference
Raising Geese, USDA Farmers' Bulletin 2251

See THE FORGOTTEN ARTS, Book One, for:

Managing the Small Woodlot

Cooking on a Wood Stove

Keeping a Family Cow

Spring Tonic: Wild Greens and How to Fix Them

Keeping a Small Flock of Chickens for Home Use

Whole Wheat Bread from Grain to Loaf

Raising and Drying Beans and Corn

Creating Natural Dyes from Common Plants

Brewing Apple Cider and Vinegar at Home

Making Plain and Fancy Soap

See THE FORGOTTEN ARTS, Book Three, for:

Making Wattle and Other Portable Fences

Reclaiming an Old Apple Tree

Drying Flowers for Winter Bouquets

Designing and Building a Grape Arbor

Weaving Baskets with Black Ash

Sharpening and Rehandling Hand Tools

Painting Colonial Patterned Floors

Making and Firing Weatherproof Bricks

Working with a Draft Horse

Root Cellars for Vegetable Storage

Yankee, Inc., Dublin, New Hampshire 03444

RICHARD M. BACON

The author and his family live as self-reliantly as possible on their small New Hampshire farm. Formerly a newspaper reporter and actor, he spent most of his professional life teaching at Collegiate School in New York City and Germantown Friends School in Philadelphia before a consuming passion for herbs and country living encouraged him to take up permanent residence and turn to farming and writing. A graduate of Williams College, he also studied in England at The London Academy of Music and Dramatic Art. He is the author of *The Forgotten Art of Growing, Gardening and Cooking with Herbs* and editor of *The Forgotten Art of Building a Stone Wall,* both published by Yankee, Inc., and has contributed articles to *Yankee, The Old Farmer's Almanac,* and *New Hampshire Profiles,* among other publications. Today, he and his family raise and process flowers for dried bouquets and sell herbs and herb products in the time left from tending a flock of sheep, geese, chickens, guinea hens, an all-purpose horse named Nellie Melba, and Maude, the family cow.